High Stepping through

the neighborhood
T.M.

High Stepping *through* the neighborhood T.M.

by Jerry Van Amerongen

Foreword by Jim Unger

Andrews and McMeel
A Universal Press Syndicate Company
Kansas City • New York

ISBN: 0-8362-1816-7

Library of Congress Catalog Card Number: 89-82504

Foreword

Jerry Van Amerongen doesn't just illustrate a gag. With his superb line work, his sense of space, design, and movement, he can take you into another world, another dimension, and show you how his mind works.

When he draws a motorcycle, he leaves nothing to chance. He draws every nut and bolt. Once he has the props right, his hilarious characters inhabit a world beyond the imagination of all but their creator. That's why he's so special.

I've met him. He's way over six feet tall, urbane and handsome as the devil.

How could anybody like a guy like that?

— JIM UNGER, creator of Herman

Support hose

Joyce is easily pleased.

There stirred within Mark a vague yearning.

Goodhue had half a notion to turn back.

What's a tamale stand doing up there,
wondered Shel.

So much for trying to ignore the animal,
thought Richard.

Only after the sneezing ended did Blair realize how snug the chair really was.

Had Ben known his wife was preparing fish, he'd have stayed in the den.

Worse yet, the guy turns out to be a bowler.

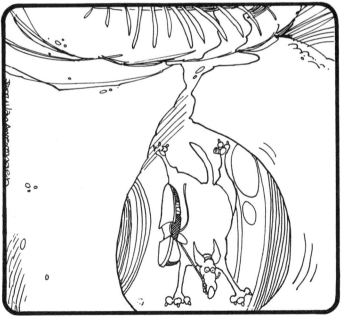

A tear wells up in the eye of shoe enthusiast
Lyle Marks.

Meanwhile, over at the cartoonists'
old age home . . .

Evidently Bob's failed in his attempt to overcome
poor thought patterns.

Artie always pretends to be surprised.

Another trout stream down the tubes.

TODAY'S QUIZ: Which person spent his time more wisely?

Given as he is to self-deception, Charles waits for a sign from the head chicken.

It's the rubber mouse that's the catalyst behind Dexter's mateless life-style.

With an honest but failing idea, Capt. Billy again casts his eyes toward the sea.

Occasionally Artie lets his turtle cut the lawn.

Elliot has the kind of dog that curls at your foot.

A cool dollop of pasta hastens Samuel to deeper thoughts.

Jason brings a note of sarcasm to his driver critiques.

Thomas is awakened by a territorial dispute.

Raymond thinks he's a houseplant.

Samuel's out front counting ants again.

Until a moment ago, Sparky never knew there was such a thing as a sliding glass door.

Keep your pet off chewing gum as long as possible.

Bob's dog appears to shy away from outboard motors of 100 hp or more.

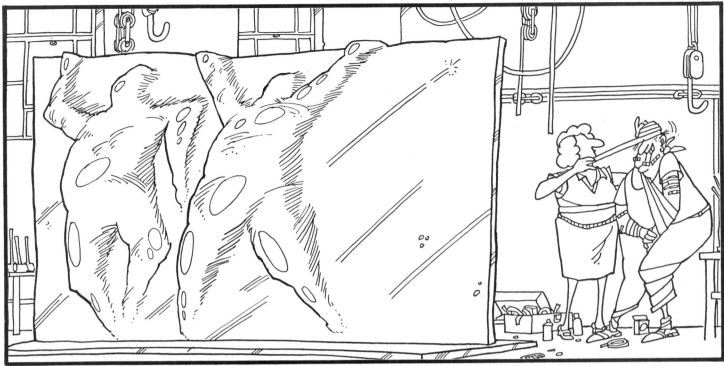

Thankfully, Elliot is nearly finished with his sculpture entitled *Three Men*.

The residue of another domestic drama

"I see you're a self-starter, Mr. Donnelly."

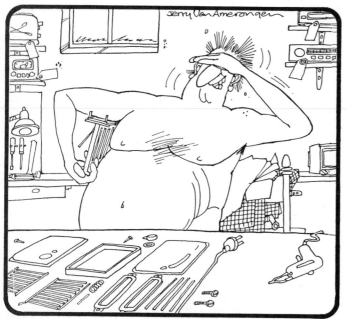

After a career spanning 1,247 electrical shocks, repairman Gary Means field-strips another toaster.

A couple of quick moves and Ed Spalding turns 10 rubber bands into a soft sculpture of George Washington.

Allen's double major was Ornithology and Home Economics.

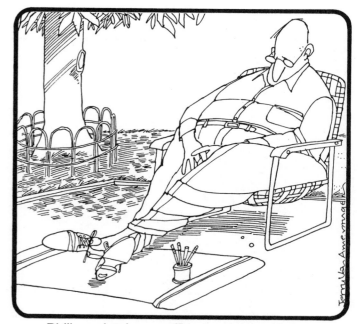

Philip maintains an office presence at home.

Elliot just dreamed he went to hell, where people spent all of their time on cheap porch furniture.

After watching the man's right turn signal blink aimlessly for just under 27 miles, Carl makes his move.

It's not the sort of thing one expects from his new accountant.

Gwenn continues to be hampered by farsightedness.

Guido maintains a constant dining environment
with tranquilizer darts.

Billy Strider's need to test the practicality of his
pants gives him a sideache.

The Dual Pianos of Carlos and Brian —
The Early Years

Leo has turned his inventive mind toward aiding
his short wife, Ann.

"Looks like you're first up, Harry."

Mr. Burphey was sorry to see Carol had responsibility for this week's office fun period.

Nordstrom disagrees.

So much for the chilled lemon beet soup.

Mrs. McGurkey proves to be a difficult luncheon companion.

Myth No. 8: Your boss will look after your interests.

Mosquito-bite tester Noland Smiley locates a particularly heavy infestation.

Bob returns from his weekly class in Superfluous Body Movements.

Gordie's Polynesian Room employs a hypnotist to bring compliance to the no-smoking section.

Why did he tie a loaded paint brush to the dog's tail? That's what Bob is asking himself.

The thrills and spills of photo-album maintenance.

The New Age comes with a vengeance to Norm's neighbor Shirley.

The theatre hits upon a cost-effective means of providing access to its balcony seating.

Household paranoia

Puppeteer extraordinaire Lyle Flanders

Meanwhile, down at the patent office, Robert answers the question, "Of what possible use?"

If it's true that every person is a universe, then Paul has a couple of significant black holes.

Raymond only audibilizes every third word while conversing.

Oh-oh, there's more than one in there!

"I'm tired, but it's a good kind of tired."

Vacation notes: Trouble in paradise

James tires of his TV dinner.

While nibbling on his toenails, Marcus experiences an involuntary leg jerk.

The inevitable fashion conclusion to the fitness craze.

Someone put a golf ball in Philip's trumpet.

First, Bobby Fitzer had six drinks, then he offered to grate the cheese.

It's a drag for Dr. Paul when folks discover he's a skin specialist.

Mr. Waverly appears to have fallen from the ledge of contentment.

Sensing the woman's hands might be cold, Ben responds.

Bob falls asleep trying to find the entrees on another one of those theme menus.

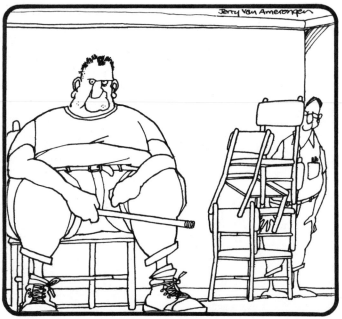

Ever mindful of the space requirements of others,
Maynard elects to stand.

Bob's celebration of his positive self spills
into the hallway.

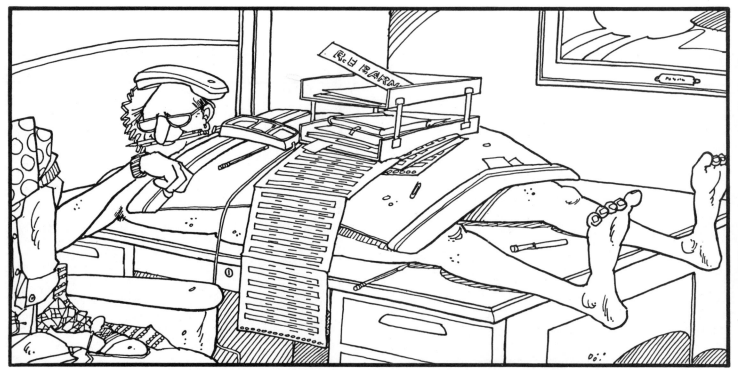

Mr. Barnie checks the time remaining in his afternoon free period.

By today's male intimacy standards, tossing a can of motor oil into your
neighbor's yard, as a get-acquainted gesture, is woefully inadequate.

Skipper pays the price for a gape-mouthed
sleeping style.

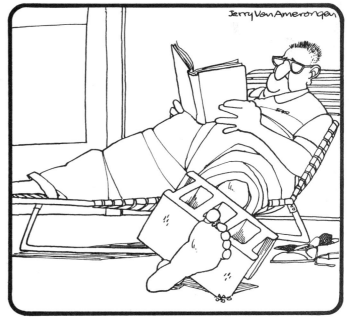

Darrell is interested in expanding
his pain threshold.

Pet therapist Marjorie Medows gives Rosco his own secret mantra.

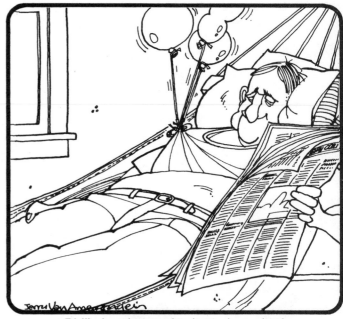

Philip has learned to be truly excited about himself.

One never nose . . . does one?!

Obviously, Ben forgot it was bowling night.

A lot of city folks think it's all work and no play in the country.

Charles has found the seam in the zone defense of life.

Mrs. Bixby just maced her husband.

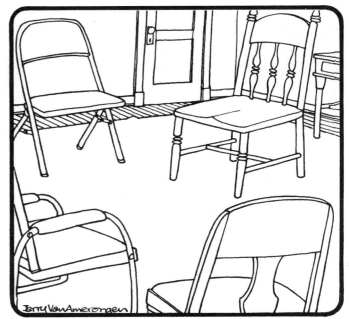

An encounter group for procrastinators.

One stupe tries to hunt butterflies off the top of the other stoop.

As an affirmation to the concept of liberty, Bob has just released his bug collection.

A well-balanced businessman

Alex was the quickest of the three men.

Sara's summer nights grow longer.

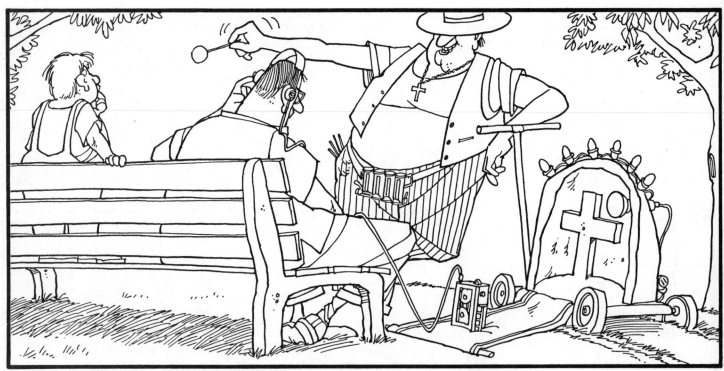

Dr. Bob professes a religion of convenience.

After a spirited match, small animal wrestler Guy Sullivan pins his hamster.

Mr. Johnson will resume his quest for inner peace after breakfast.

Audio-visual technology is the next logical course for Seymour.

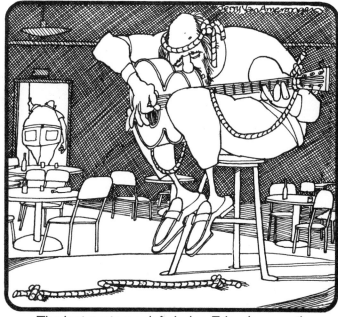

The last customer left during Edger's seventh song, which was also about rope.

Two tall people check out of a hotel that boasts of a ceiling fan in every room.

Were Bud more observant, he wouldn't be fretting just now about his hearing.

The fish company's 17th-floor location is a big part of its promotional activities.

Philip feels responsible for all behavior within his immediate vicinity.

Gary suffers an emotional bushwhacking.

Hail the size of elephants

Miss Vicki will figure prominently in Sid's afternoon.

Well, that's it for fall.

Cutting the grass on Maynard Selby Point.

The Filger brothers communicate with each other through tiny radios on their wrists.

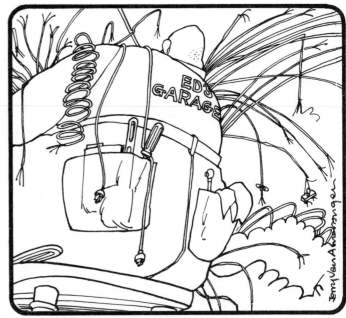

Carlos pauses to assess his chances with Mr. Armbruster's electronic ignition system.

Another Postal Department training session, designed to teach younger employees how to ignore long lines of customers.

Thomas Avery's recurring fear is that his brain will get real small and fall out of his right ear.

Gloria's looking to propel herself out of the relationship.

Raymond puts a stop to his critical inner dialogue.

Brice would be considered your heavy-handed worm hunter.

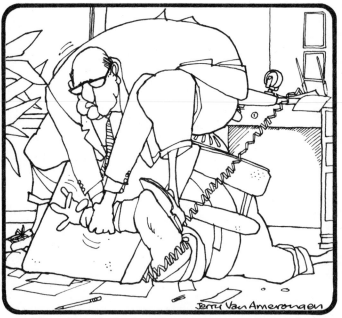

Then there's the hands-on management style.

After years of negotiating the sharp curves of business, Nester's brakes are fading.

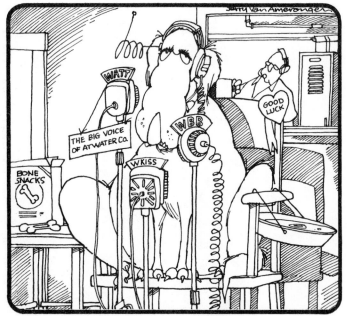

The "Call-In-and-Bark-at-Sparky Show" during a recent three-county hookup

Cynthia comes face to face with the possibility that brains may be self-cleaning.

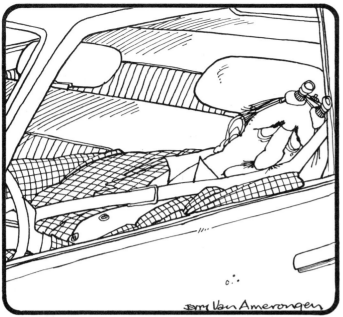

High-rise analyst Drew Hillary takes a break.

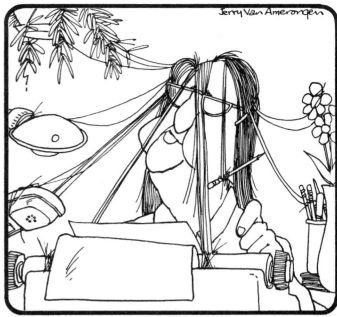

Susan is soon caught up in her work.

Jonathan brings a sense of symmetry
to his writing.

And so the city begins to take its toll on Francis.

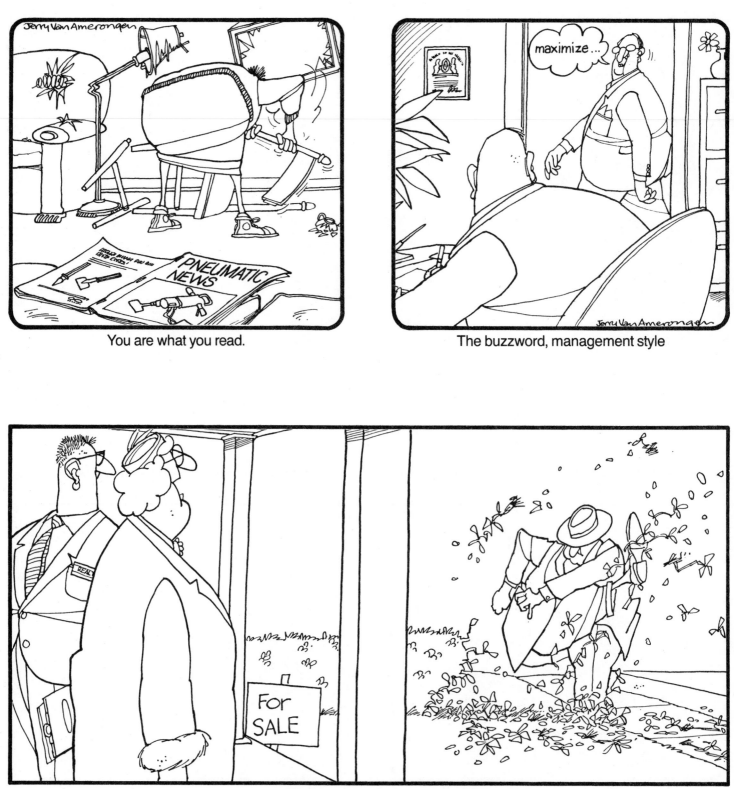

You are what you read.

The buzzword, management style

"Edward, if we buy it, you can do something with the hedge!"

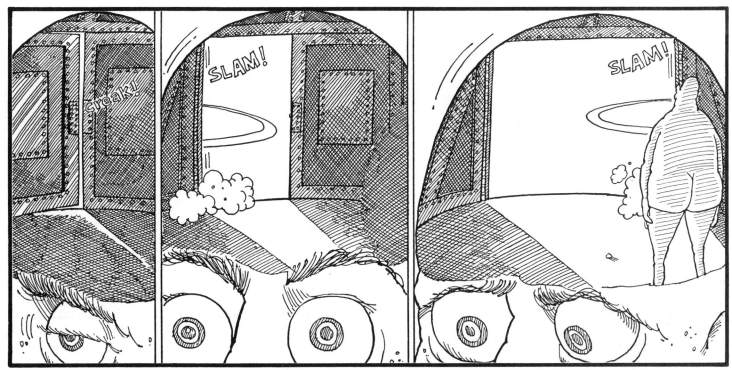

A sudden realization (with some shame attached)

Carl is a person who has trouble with the democratic process.

At this very moment, Claudia's odometer matches up perfectly with her zip code.

After mulling over the possibility of sharing his
peace and quiet with the Frisbee,
Eugene makes his move.

If it's true that socks are a barometer of the man,
Philip should forget about the bus and begin
walking, immediately.

Another minimally exceptional person

Jane and Roger's boundaries collapse.

Bill and Elaine Cleever were the first to recognize Paterson, N.J. as the birthplace of Chicken Chow Mein.

It's Aaron's view that the heft and balance of one's utensil adds immeasurably to one's dining experience.

A sure sign

With Hadley, what you see is what you get.

I think I saw that guy at the hosiery sale, thought Ted.

The right pet could take your mind off a troublesome day.

Bob sorts through the complex web of human interactions.

At some point in a long-term relationship, there's a parting of mutual interests.

Expectation gives way to reality.

At the Earthworm Research Center

Warren is neither rock-solid nor market-wise.

Ben never gives tactile responsibilities to his upper extremities.

Harness racing: the early years

Another animal trainer abuses his position.

Shawn rides the high plateau of the
emotional landscape.

Art critic viewing an impertinent little painting.

This year's Irrational Fears Grand Champion worries, from her home in Madison, Wis., about being caught up in a deadly lava flow.

Edwin's slow drift from the accepted norms of society gathered steam with the acquisition of the papier-mache kangaroo tail.

Bob and Shirley have been together a long time.

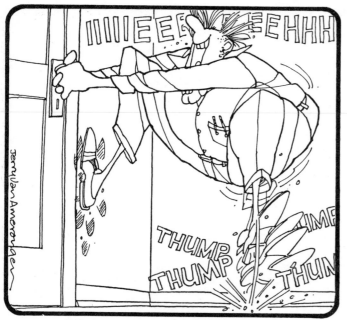

Billy lost his second-floor apartment
within a week.

"Impostor" is the word that creeps into
Mr. Markey's mind.

Jason is strong on "How" and weak on "Why."

"Tomorrow, how about I slip out and
get a flyswatter . . ."

Connie is a mass of contradictions.

Barriers trigger within Fredric a primal sense of freedom.

An ability to think clearly would only spoil the symmetry of Colleen's life.

Eddie the Revealer is about to add an element of urgency to the council's anti-obscenity debate.

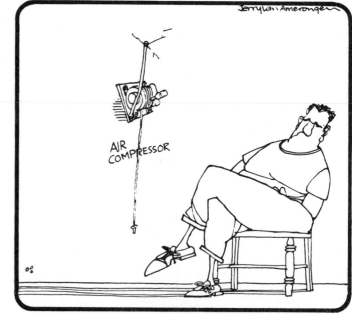

Posed before his "wall of meaningful things," we come face to face with Aaron's simplistic nature.

Phyllis remains unimpressed.

Mr. Claybourne's out of plumb today.

Another person, living a life of continuous and never-ending, stringent self-examination.

Another Personality Test that's managed to substantiate Morton's bent towards cynicism.

Bob exercises extremely poor judgment.

Larry just had a brainstorm.

Based on Stan's self-assured countenance, he's obviously forgotten he's still in his work clothes.

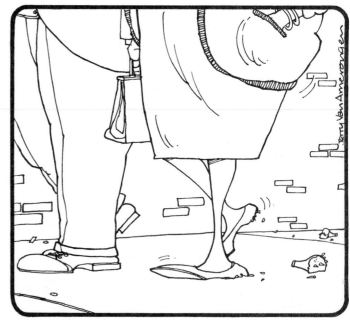

"That's odd," thought Trisha, as she glanced over at Bernard, "I don't remember him being that tall."

Upon leaving the club in full regalia, it was Bob's misfortune to encounter a very large bird dog.

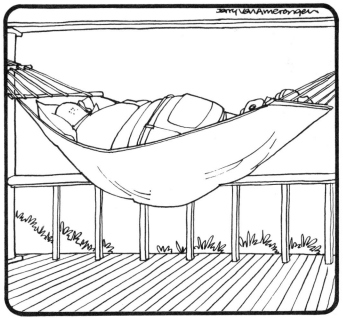

Some years back, Brad decided to stop by the side of the road and just think about where everyone else was going.

Mr. Smiley attempts to scuff off some of his forward momentum.

The exploration of reality ended for Neal with the acquisition of the fish.

That's when Jerome realized he wasn't alone on the court.

The efficiency of the beater ejection system leaves Carl speechless.

Raymond's dog is trained to eat the lining out of cheap suits.

Alex made his attaché case entirely of clothespins.

Bob encounters a belligerent frogman.

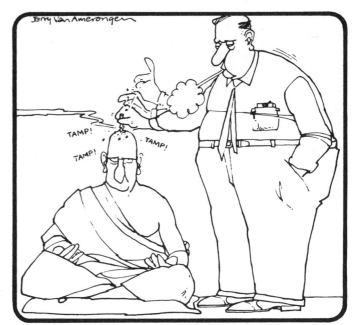

Raymond doesn't hold contemplation in high regard.

"I feel I should warn you, my Arthur likes to keep the games moving along."

Why they never run out of dark meat down at Shelley's Deli.

You wouldn't want to be in a hurry and run into Billy Skuggs.

A kind of low-grade gas is being given off by Mr. Kerney's new wallpaper.

Bernie has trouble coming down from his fishing trips.

"That's all right, Emilio. It's the Hendersons."

Carl is reminded of the ban on cigar smoking.

Bradley knocks the formality out of wearing a cummerbund.

Mrs. Gerkey comes down from her afternoon soap.

Carl attempts to enhance his margin for error.

"Say, I couldn't help noticing your rabbits seem awful skittish . . ."

Bernard Hillary is a close observer of the human defensive reflex.

Delores sheds the ceremonial
garb of contentment.

Remembering other times, Carl takes
a Sunday drive.

Eric the Tolerant

Claire loses her struggle with subtlety.

Once a month or so some of the guys get together over at Ray's, have a bite
to eat, and fight a small grass fire.

Another major dude

Roy and Stephen form the letter "K."

Wow, thought Bennett, anticipating the conversation and fellowship possibilities to come.

Before their evening stroll, Marcia thought Gilbert only *LOOKED* like a cheap flamenco dancer.

Mr. Beaker does a little corporate downsizing on Samuelson.

Emerson dabbles with his new body-cleansing system.

The all-new continuing adventure series now running in
Seating Illustrated magazine

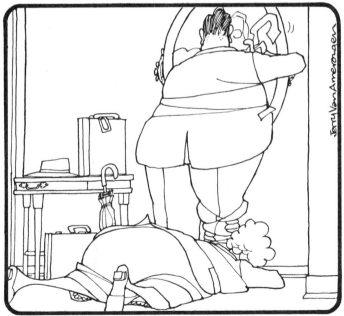

Shelley doesn't want to be a
career woman anymore.

Eugene's brain made him drape old radio parts
about his person.

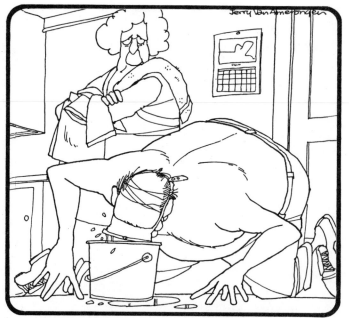

And so, Mason begins his slow, arduous trek
toward a career as a deep-sea diver.

It's got something to do with Helen's muddled
notion about a common value among
all living things.

Ah, there's a town!...punctuated by
inexpensive eateries, but if
you pick an expensive eatery
it'll cost ya more...

Philip takes pride in being a generalist.

Gregory designs his own Formica furniture.

Elliot goes from one rural antique store to another, seeking approval from perfect strangers.

Actually, after being so quick to say no, Gracy did find a brush or two she could use.

Another unpleasantness

"Come away from the tools, Eugene!"

So it's not the corn after all, thought Mason.

To better stem the flow of nonproductivity,
Caroline Velcros her hand to the desk.

Neither Carl nor Eric will be invited back.

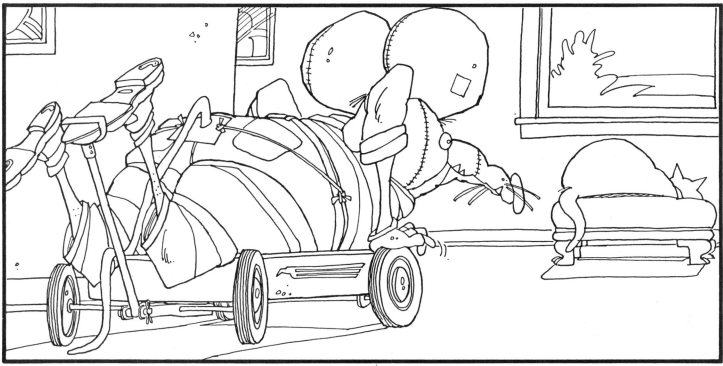

Time to exercise the cat.

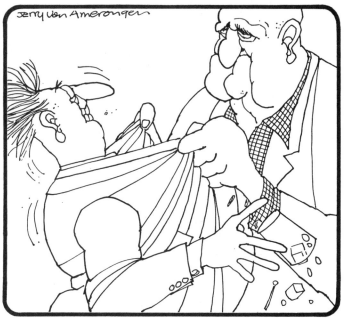

Carl wipes the smirk off the face of give and take.

Gloria's been dreaming about putting up
new wallpaper.

Alex uses his art to get in touch with a troubled childhood.

Mr. G. mistreated a number of his people at the office today.

Another couple fine-tuning their relationship.

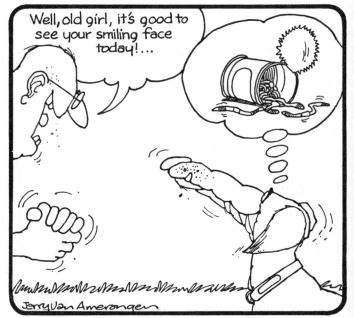

It's a wonder we get along as well as we do.

The pervasive influences of living
too close together

As usual, aggressive behavior sets the dog off.

Eric involves Mr. Bingham in his territorial issues.

Walking a relish tray through
a tough neighborhood.

There's nothing quite so pathetic as a relish enthusiast whose contribution goes untouched.

Mindful of slipping into old family patterns, Edward uses his visit to alter the chemistry.

Lunch with supportive friends

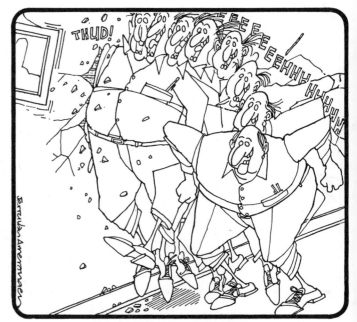

Brian lacks emotional fitness.

Plumage is a recurring theme in David's life.

"Oh great! Now we'll be late for sure!"

Kevin manages to mix athletics with partying.

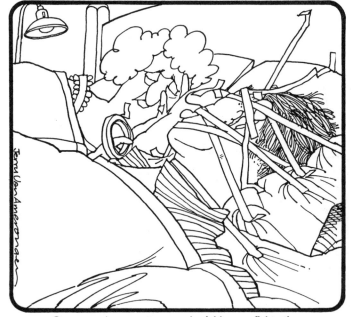

Gregory knew at once he'd been fidgeting
in his sleep.

Philip supports the adage, "We teach what we most need to learn."

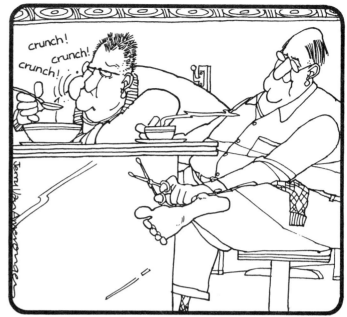

Try telling Daniel toenails are of little use.

Garrett cleans out another emotional closet.

The winner of the "Zippers and Me" essay contest

Being new to international travel, Earl enunciates carefully so the Canadian couple might better understand.

Paul's observational skills remain underdeveloped.

Paul forgot his mantra.

Not recommended for nonprofessionals

Probing the outer perimeter of merchandising

Local TV news finds its market.

The ever-shifting dynamics of married life

"Say, those nuts look pretty tasty!"

The first red flag of the evening

Chip leaves the Cycling Club.

True, the fellow across the aisle has his shoe in his pocket, but Jason wonders if he shouldn't introduce himself just the same.

Here's a little something you might want to try the next time your doctor leaves you abandoned in one of those little beige-colored examination rooms.

Michael receives a casual introduction.

Another theme dinner over at the Snyders'

Even though her husband's been a "pill" all afternoon, Alice protects him from a bothersome fly by smothering it with a piece of cake.

Weather forecasters in Jason's viewing area must assume some responsibility for his keen interest in the concepts of "partly cloudy-partly sunny."

The running of the bulls near Dexter, Iowa

"My foot is shrinking," thought Glenn.

Don't ya get the feeling Carl's gonna wish he hadn't worn his 100 percent wool sweater?

The idea of "doing it yourself" is a new one for Edwin.

Mr. Burphey hates to be controlled.

Clifford is struck by the notion that others live lives completely
different from his.

Bobby is lavishly endowed with life's force.

Office politics

Gail's farsightedness taps into Bob's playfulness.

Robert's the kind of guy who's completely stumped by life, but doesn't know it.

Arlene's last day on the job featured a heightened display of inventiveness.

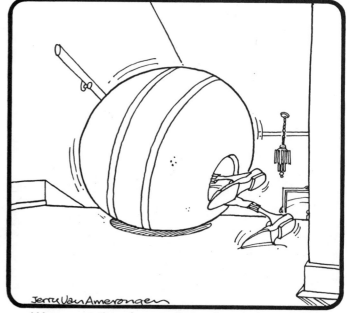

Worse yet, there're a couple of guys downstairs dressed as mallets.

Graham is an easy winner in the "period" category.

Suddenly, Artie finds himself looking down the barrel of normal life.

Marshall brings a sense of anticipation to his daily life.

Gloria makes another entry in her emotional diary.

Mr. Carlisle allows his wife to finish his sentences, so he might further assimilate the meaning of his discourse.

"Can a person have too many knick-knacks? . . . No," thought Gayland with assuredness.

Another incredibly literal person

Stephen is a crowd-control enthusiast.

Unfortunately, Cynthia discovered a majority of the judges raised ferrets,
not carrots.

IRONY

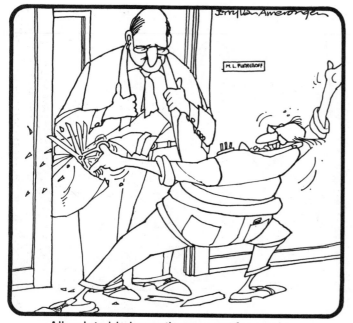

Allen lets his impertinence out for a romp.

"Excuse me, gentlemen! . . .Excuse me!"

Gretchen stands poised on the edge of
social involvement.

From time to time Gregory likes to bring Scooter
up to speed.

Another load of laundry

Warren settles into his favorite chair.

More funny business down at the club

Another of life's prophetic moments

Philip uses his report as a sort of
refreshment tent.

Gail keeps tabs on Michael when he's outside.

Carolyn conducts a relationship inventory.

Gilbert's pet suffers a disciplinary breakdown.

From the ridge of conceit, Graham takes in the broad plain of mediocrity.

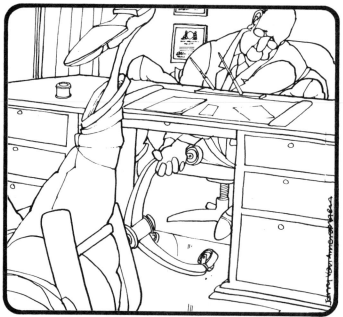

Brian went almost instantly from the disappointment of not getting his raise, to wondering if the coasters on his boss's chair made it as tipsy as the one in his office.

Because another motorist chose to take more than his share of parking spaces, Nathan chose to hammer his hubcaps into tiny, compact balls.

Taxidermy in public places

Cliff is a casual sort of guy.

Evan is about to let us in on a little secret.

Lunch begins badly for Kenny.

Cynthia finally grasps the concept.

Shelly puts birdseed on his nose.

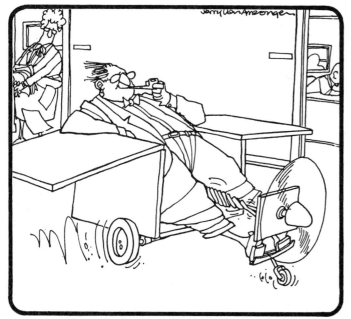

It's Billingham from down in Development.

No. 1 in the Mad Waiter series

So! . . . thought Roy.

Edwin was sorry he asked.

"I said duck, not ducks."

Sparky heard the strange noises, too.

By mid-afternoon Brian's love affair with the sun reaches a crescendo.

Preassigned seating means absolutely nothing to some people.

Howard exhibits the first signs of
job-related stress.

Somebody rubbed Jason's socks with raw meat.

The Randells reminisce with their son, Carl, about all of the stubbed toes he had as a child.

When his wife leaves the house, Mr. Wilson has difficulty feigning affection for the cat.

Tired of small talk, Edwin tries big talk.

Another unsupervised upbringing

"Toast and jam, be watchful and wary, and ready to scram." The old fortune-teller's parting poem continued to amuse Walter.

Whenever Elizabeth sees a really nice sunset, she sings the finale to "New York, New York."

Another thematic relationship

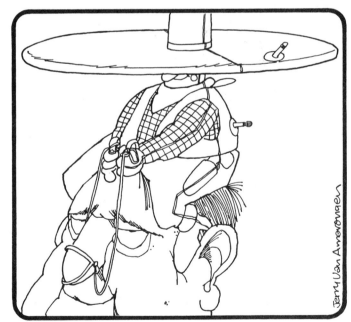

An inflatable cowboy hat

Mrs. Manley's new perfume is making Mr. Manley wonder if his engine isn't processing its fuel properly.

Gordon can't understand why so many people are upset over teeny-weeny newspaper comics.

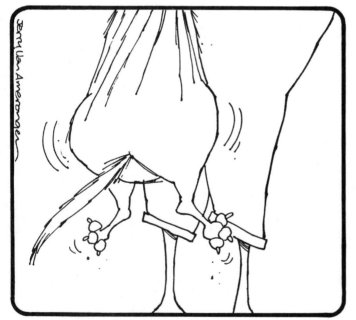

Mr. Chambers has a word with Skippy.

Victor's opinions aren't widely held.

Out of sight, out of mind

By crafting such a remarkable likeness of his mortgage banker, Paul was able to reap even greater therapeutic value.

Brad bent over to get the paper and just kept going.

Sammy thinks he's gonna like his new accountant.

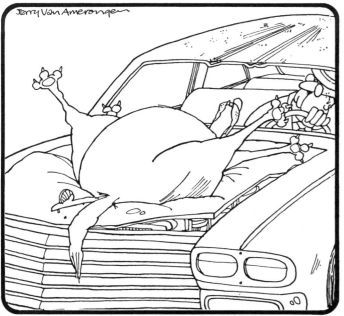

The annoying pitter-patter on the roof took form at
Doug's first complete stop.

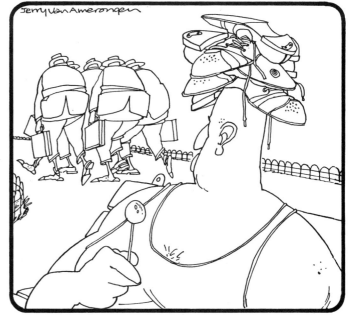

Businessmen marking another nonparticipant

. . . and that's why Uncle Carl stopped
doing birdcalls.

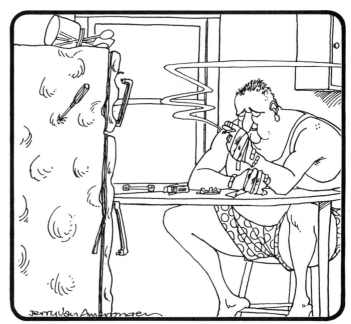

Arnie has yet to come to terms
with his refrigerator.

Ben lives in an "Up With People" environment.

After being made to wait interminably, Neal huddles with his response advisor.

Jason blows another hour of therapy.

"We better have a look at those brakes, too."

Fooled by another vague company name.

Arthur's party takes a dramatic turn.

Humor expert developing an opinion.

The tour bus's muffled sound system adds to the already disquieting ride.

The overriding concept of the bumper cars is lost on Phyllis.

Marriage to Cynthia is like being on one long retreat.

At home with a wildlife-management professional

The final strokes of Bobby Monroe's painting career

The hazards of serenading a wood-carver's daughter

Like so many of Shelley's small accidents, injury is doubtful but humiliation continual.

No wonder Bob never gets a good heart-rate up on those walks of his.

Learning to identify self-destructive tendencies

Wilson Donnelly was one of the first to discover the Maple St. flyway.

Nor, it seems, is Mitch particularly well suited for patio-furniture sales.

Edwin waxes eloquently with reasonably average observations.

How they train fast-talking automobile pitchmen.

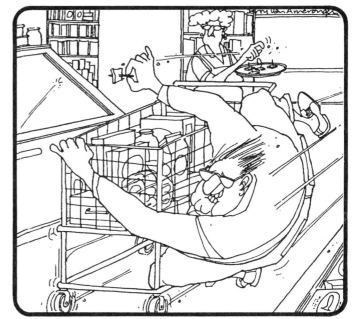

Garrett enjoys the free samples, but attempts to duck any obligation to buy.

Would the others notice he was having a little trouble again this morning? Boyd hoped not.

Elizabeth meets new men by suggesting she's not strong enough to twist the tops off her carrots.

Tough questions will no doubt be asked of Gordie, the "cable release" man.

No faint praise, coming from Jean the Pea Queen

Suddenly there was a great deal of hoopla at the next table.

It takes Elliot a while to feel like he's really on vacation.

As a kind of artistic challenge, sign painter
R.B. Chalmers has decided to jump from door
to door, lettering each tenant's name from
wherever he lands.

Male model, Harrison Derek, is led to safety after
addressing the Independent Cement Contractors
Assn. on the rigors of being a male model.

Men who know their salmon.

Another slow night at the Cafe del Sol

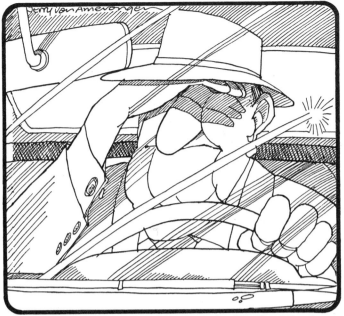

The bumper sticker ahead reads, "Retired Sock Collectors for Tranquility," and hard-driving Neal Sage knows he's picked the wrong lane again.

There's nothing quite so pathetic as a person who loses a contest which they felt with all their heart, they should have won.

Alex is a plasterman's nightmare.

Mr. Sanders decides to try another bench.

The purpose of the evening's meeting is to discuss the low overhang in the basement.

At the end of the last corridor at the National Franchise Show

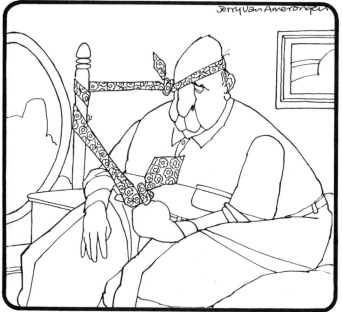

Inner direction is this morning's missing ingredient.

Behind the posturing of the casual observer

Susan's days are built upon a series of short-term goals.

Cliff moves ever closer to the creation of a really fast bluegill.

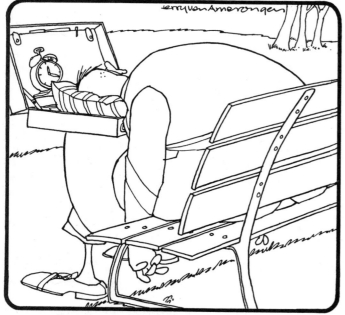

People who nap last longer, that's what Warren thinks.

Joel is the Ornamental Lamp Society's most active member.

Nowhere in the caterpillar's tangle of nerve impulses was the message formulated that one Eddie Flicky was purposely dropping seeds on its head.

It has something to do with Edwin's fears that his pet, being domesticated, no longer associates eating with food gathering in the wild.

Gracie's fear of driving in reverse isn't entirely unfounded.

A kind of *THOROUGHNESS* during Ed's pamphlet-distribution years is now a kind of *MADNESS* during his butcher years.

Believing humor to be the shortest distance between two people, Cliff prepares to mingle.

Conscientious corporate smoker

The first day of fly-fishing school

The book that changed Philip's life

Edwin is losing some of his spontaneity.

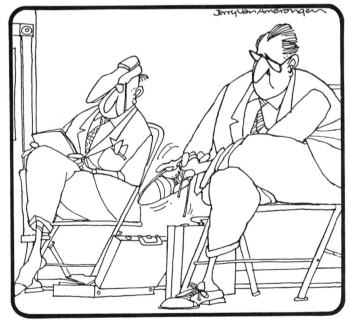

Most of us are capable of absorbing the negative
suggestions of others.

Wilson soon discovers how the restaurant assigns tables to its waiters.

You'll never find Philip very far from nature.

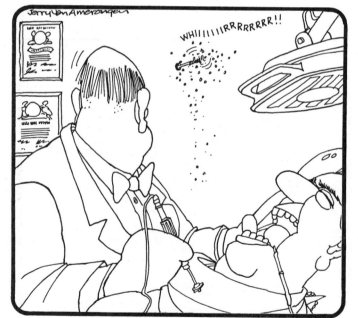

Oh-oh, Dr. Bill's left a patient waiting in the other chair too long.

The Hemalshots took in another terrific party last night.

Bob's choice of decor gives customers a better feeling about their purchase.

So much for trying to eat a wholesome cereal
in a natural setting.

Kyle should never have given the stylist free rein.

Sparky's posturing for dominance ends
on a sour note.

Anton uses a hair dryer to give his birds
a robust look.

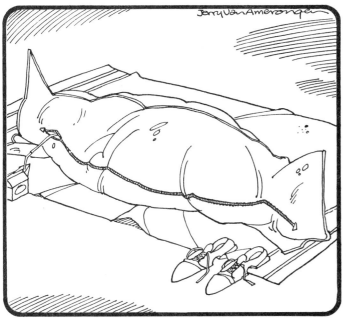

At home with coping specialist Aaron Sibley.

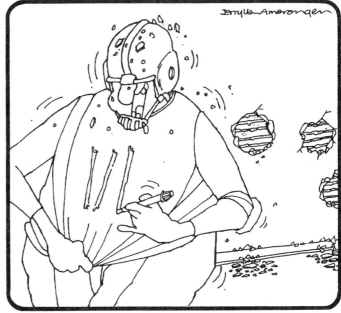

Philip goes through a bottle of aspirin a week.

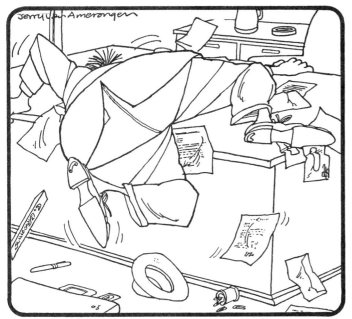

Ropes-course participant, Carl Sturgess, transfers his experience to the office.

Bob dabbles with the concept of performance art.

Sparky's dream suddenly changes from chasing a cat to being chased by a plant.

The chef should never have accepted Allen's soup order.

New doubts about beavers as backyard playmates

Connie's communal responsibilities know no bounds.

Samuel has an imaginary business partner.

The devious widow Cartwright sets her sights on Bill.

Evidently Skipper feels it's Mr. Dibble's turn
to let him out.

Ed Hurley tests motion-sickness bags for
a major airline.

This, of course, does nothing to allay Philip's
concerns about the milkman.

Meredith can never understand all the fuss about
not being able to find a ripe melon.

Tiny little bells on the inside are the cause of
Eddie's tiny little bells on the outside.

Mr. Billinger takes a little of the muscle out of
his power breakfast.

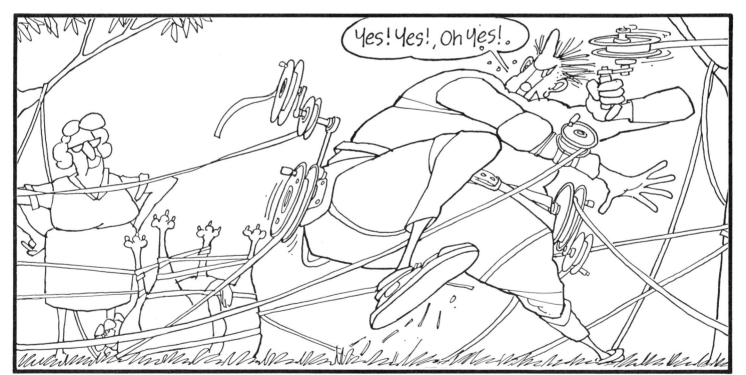

Yes! Yes!, Oh Yes!.

On Monday, Alice is gonna ask the folks down at the hardware store to keep
all their masking tape under the counter.

Susan was able to show Miss Mars her criticism of the blender's reliability was groundless.

Marcia's departure was something more than a speck on Eric's emotional windshield.

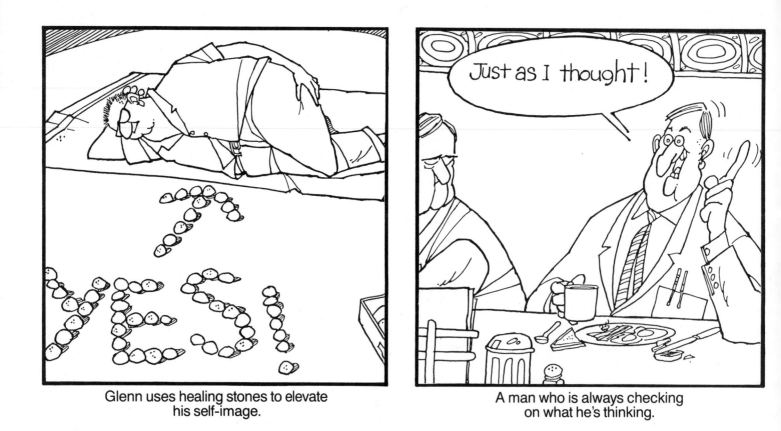

Glenn uses healing stones to elevate
his self-image.

A man who is always checking
on what he's thinking.

How many of us believe Jeffrey spends too much time with the dog?

Three more victims of "job-related shame."

Gary's powers of recall are truly pathetic.

Carrie dreams fussy little dreams.